1 MONTH OF
FREE
READING

at

www.ForgottenBooks.com

By purchasing this book you are eligible for one month membership to ForgottenBooks.com, giving you unlimited access to our entire collection of over 1,000,000 titles via our web site and mobile apps.

To claim your free month visit: www.forgottenbooks.com/free1041612

ISBN 978-0-331-24394-9
PIBN 11041612

WOODLAWN GARDENS
GLADIOLUS

E. C. SWARTLEY   STERLING, ILLINOIS

HAVE A HOBBY—GROW SOME GLADS

A SQUARE DEAL TO ALL
ORGANIZED 1913

THE GLADIOLUS

IN the history of the flora world there have been very few varieties which have become so popular as the gladiolus. You perhaps can recall quite a few years ago, the gladiolus grown by our grandmothers, a small red or yellow bloom. That would be an insignificant thing compared with our modern "glad," with blooms from four to six inches across, and as many as twelve blooms open at a time.

Its great variety of colors, ease of culture, immunity from disease and long keeping qualities as a cut flower, place the Gladiolus at the head of the list for garden culture, and for the many other purposes flowers are used.

This catalog contains the names and descriptions of more than 125 varieties, and while all of them are not new, they are the worth-while varieties selected from over 200 we have had on trial. We cannot grow all of the varieties, (of which there are over two thousand), but our aim is to grow the best of them.

WE GUARANTEE SATISFACTION

This means that the bulbs will be of satisfactory size (1¼ inches in diameter, or over), finest quality and well packed. They must be true to name and healthy. If, for any reason, bulbs do not please you, tell us before you tell your neighbor. Then you won't have to tell him. No grower is immune from making an occasional error, but any mistakes we may make will be adjusted to your satisfaction.

A HOBBY THAT GREW

To our many friends who visited our gardens, and to the hundreds of customers from all parts of the United States, we owe our success in developing a hobby that has grown to considerable proportions, and we expect to plant this season nearly a million bulbs and about 200 varieties.

We wish to thank all of our kind friends who so ably assisted us in increasing our sales, and we want you to know that we fully appreciate your kindness. You are cordially invited to visit us any time, tho from late July until about September 10th you will find nearly all of our varieties in bloom.

CULTURAL DIRECTIONS

THE following is prepared for the benefit of the novice:

We believe gladiolus will do well in any soil that will produce a good crop of corn or potatoes. A fertile soil will undoubtedly give better results in size of bloom, and also produce a larger bulb. A little extra care in cultivation and fertilization will amply repay you. *DO NOT USE* fresh manure before planting bulbs. Manure shoull be applied in the Fall. Very scabby bulbs will be the result of fresh manure.

DEPTH TO PLANT

We would suggest planting bulbs from four to five inches deep. Don't guess, but measure the depth. A bulb will grow as well planted much shallower, but bulbs planted deep are protected from falling over, which often occurs with tall growing varieties.

SUBSTITUTIONS

Many varieties are in great demand and we advise placing orders early to avoid disappointments. We do not substitute unless requested to do so, but we reserve the privilege of giving you two one-inch bulbs instead of one larger size, in case we are unable to furnish the large size.

DISCOUNTS

A discount of 5% in bulbs will be allowed on all cash orders of $5.00 or over, and 10% in bulbs on orders of $10.00 or more. The extra bulbs given as discounts can be the customer's choice if so desired. Orders for less than $1.00 not accepted.

	EACH	DOZEN

ALBANIA (Kemp) .... $ .15 $1.50
　　Purest glistening white. Extra good commercial vari-
　　ety. Ruffled

ALICE TIPLADY (Kunderd)............................... .10 1.00
　　Bittersweet pink, suffused scarlet at outer edges, and
　　reverse, throat buff yellow. One of the best in the
　　orange shades. A fine cut flower variety.

AMERICAN BEAUTY (Diener)............................ .25 2.50
　　An attractive American beauty color. Throat creamy
　　yellow, striped with ruby. Flowers large and many
　　open at one time.

ANNIE EBERIUS (Diener).................................. .15 1.50
　　Deep Rhomadine purple, shading into a very deep bor-
　　deaux center. An extremely attractive variety of ex-
　　ceptional merit.

ADELINE KENT (Diener).................................. .20 2.00
　　An intensely ruffled variety of good size, of a soft rose
　　pink color. Lovers of the ruffled type will like this
　　one.

ALTON (Kunderd) .... .15 1.50
　　An exceptionally fine ruffled variety of a distinct
　　orange shade. A beauty.

ADORATION .... .15 1.50
　　A very attractive flower, deep pink, with a tinge of
　　blue on edge of petals.

ARABIA (Holland) ....
　　Refer to PERSIA for description.

BENGAL TIGER (Pratt).................................. .20 2.00
　　In color and stripes, it resembles its name. You will
　　be more than pleased with this one.

BYRON SMITH (Kunderd)............................... .10 1.00
　　Light lavender, delicately suffused mallow purple,
　　deeper at edge of petals. Throat a light yellow with
　　etchings of mallow purple at base. I consider this the
　　best of the light lavender class.

BUCKEYE (Kunderd) .... .15 1.50
　　Very large dark pink, darker spot in the throat.

BLUE JAY (Graff).. .20 2.00
　　This variety comes nearly being a true blue with a
　　pure white spot in throat. Extremely popular.

BREAK O' DAY (Bill).................................... 2.50
　　A new one, pink blossoms with soft, creamy yellow
　　blotch on lower petals. Outstanding on account of
　　its earliness.

CHATEAU THIERRY

DESCRIPTION ON PAGE FIVE

	EACH	DOZEN
CARMEN SYLVIA (Prestgard)	$ .15	$1.50

CARMEN SYLVIA (Prestgard).............................$ .15 $1.50
This is an exceptionally fine white, large blooms, six
open at once. Fine commercial variety.

CRIMSON GLOW (Betscher)......................... .10 1.00
Beautiful, rich glowing crimson. Few can equal it in
its color.

CRINKLES (Diener) .... .35 3.50
Deep peach-blossom pink. It is intensely ruffled and
resembles a double hollyhock. Extra fine.

CHATEAU THIERRY (Vos)......................... .15 1.50
Bright cerise, a red blotch bordered with yellow on
lower petals. Resembles Hollywood very much.

DR. ELKINS (Kunderd)......................... .25 2.50
A true sport of Mrs. Frank Pendleton. Same large
and showy flower, but the original rose pink has
changed to white with large throat blotches of a fine
shade of lilac blue.

DR. W. VAN FLEET (Diener)......................... .15 1.50
Tall, very early, a magnificent shade of delicate rose-
pink. A general favorite.

DESDEMONE (Vilmoin) .... .50 5.00
Perhaps this variety is the most unusual color of any
variety we are growing. Ashy-rose, striped lilac, large
dark red blotch edged ivory white. Immense spike of
large double row of flowers. With this variety in
your garden you will be the envy of all your friends.

DORRITT (Kunderd) .... .25 2.50
Very large mottled, or speckled, deep pink. Very
attractive and the equal of Detroit, which it resembles
in coloring.

DUCHESS OF YORK (Holland)......................... .25 2.50
Large flowers of a purple blue color. Seedling of
Baron Jos. Hulot. Vigorous grower and good multi-
plier.

E. J. SHAYLOR (Kunderd)......................... .10 1.00
Large ruffled blossoms of a beautiful pure, deep, rose-
pink, on tall spikes.

ELIZABETH GERBERDING (Diener)......................... .15 1.50
Shell pink, heavily ruffled, shading into rose on the
outer edges. Center, pale canary and ruby. A very
nice ruffled flower.

ELIZABETH TABOR

DESCRIPTION ON PAGE SEVEN

	EACH	DOZEN

ELIZABETH TABOR (Hinkle)..............................$ .15 $1.50
> Winner of the first prize as the best new commercial
> variety in 1923.   Extremely early, blooming in 60
> days.   Petals are a delicate rose-pink on white ground,
> lower ones bearing a rich dark crimson blotch, term-
> inating in a diamond of soft yellow.

EMILY ASHE (Kunderd)..................................... .25 2.50
> In my opinion, a poor white, though very nicely ruf-
> fled.. Blossoms of medium size. Small cerise blotch
> on lower petals.

ETENDARD (Lemoine) .... .15 1.50
> A cream-white, French variety, with large, bright red
> center. A very beautiful and attractive variety.

ELIZABETH SWARTLEY (Swartley)............................... 5.00
> Named in memory of our mother. Color, a beautiful
> soft LaFrance pink blending into a milk-white throat.
> Its outstanding feature is its unusual color, never be-
> fore seen in an early variety. We predict it will be-
> come one of the most popular commercial varieties of
> recent introduction. Stock limited.

EUGENE LEFEBRE (Lemoine)........................... .25 2.50
> An exceptionally fine French variety.   Deep pink,
> with throat blotched purpleish Amaranth and cream.
> You will miss a beauty if you fail to get this one.

EVELYN KIRTLAND (Austin)........................... .10 1.00
> Rose-pink in color, with darker edges. Brilliant scar-
> let blotches on lower petals. Entire flower casts a
> glistening, sparkling luster. Very large flowers on a
> giant spike. A beautiful decorative variety.

ELF (Diener) .... .15 1.50
> Lemon yellow buds, opening into snow-white flowers
> with lemon yellow lip. A perfect blend of two colors.

EXQUISITE (Kunderd) .... .25 2.50
> An exceptionally fine glad of true American Beauty
> rose color, and all that its name implies.

ELKHART .... .25 2.50

EUROPEA (Pfitzer) .... .10 1.00
> Snow-white, without a trace of color. One of the most
> beautiful whites.

	EACH	DOZEN
FIRE RIBBON (Kunderd)	$ .20	$2.00

Tall, with many blooms open at one time. The spike is a lone, fiery band of glowing red. Exceedingly rich, and strikingly showy.

FERN KYLE (Kunderd) .... .50   5.00

Palest cream with primrose colored throat. Very nicely ruffled and a winner in any company. A beauty.

FLORA (Velthny's) .... .10   1.00

A fine canary yellow, second only to Golden Measure. Best yellow for the price. Flower four inches in diameter. Strong, healthy grower.

GIANT NYMPH (Coleman) .... .25   2.50

LaFrance pink with creamy yellow throat. Very large, wide open flowers, well arranged on stem. This is without doubt one of the very best of recent introductions.

GLENDALE (Davis Shelby) .... .15   1.50

American beauty red, a trifle darker than American beauty rose. Fine.

GOLD (Decorah Glad Gardens) .... .20   2.00

Pure golden yellow. A fine, clear self yellow. Perhaps the best yellow to date, and in my opinion is the finest florist yellow ever introduced.

GOLDEN MEASURE (Kelway) .... .15   1.50

Straw yellow, lower petals suffused amber yellow. Large flowers and very vigorous grower.

GIANT MYRTLE .... .25   2.50

Soft pink on white ground. Large flower on long spike. Beautifully dainty.

GLADYS PLATHE (Diener) .... .20   2.00

Orchid flowering, lilac and red velvet blotches. Large flowers and a beautiful variety.

GOLDEN KING (Blads) .... .15   1.50

Clear, unfading yellow with a vivid crimson blotch in the throat. The flowers are good sized, well opened and well spaced on strong, straight spikes.

GOSHEN (Kunderd) .... .20   2.00

A fine flower of medium deep silvery rose-pink color. Large, showy rose-red blotches. Very good.

GLORY OF KENNEMERLAND (Holland) .... .10   1.00

This is a very unusual flower. It is a very rich deep rose, with golden yellow blotch in throat. Flower very large, wide open bell-shaped, with rounded petals.

	EACH	DOZEN

HALLEY (Velthnys) ....$ .06 $ .60
> Delicate, salmon pink, with creamy blotch and darker stripes on lower petals. A very early bloomer.

HELGA (Kunderd) .... .15 1.50
> Fine salmon rose. Deeper rose and cream on white ground. A great improvement over Halley, which it somewhat resembles.

HERADA (Austin) .... .10 1.00
> A beautiful sparkling mauve, with deeper shadings in throat. Very unusual and attractive color, and a general favorite.

HOOSIER (Kunderd) .... .20 2.00
> A giant flower of finest salmon rose. Throat blotches as large and as beautiful as in Mrs. Frank Pendleton. Color of blotches violet maroon.

HENRY C. GOEHL (Fischer)............................... .25 2.50
> Large, open, creamy white flowers, with a beautiful red blotch. A new and wonderful variety.

HOLLYWOOD (Shelley) .... .35 3.50
> Beautiful, big scarlet blossoms, with gorgeous yellow throats. Tall spikes, and a wonderfully striking variety.

HELEN FRANKLIN (Kunderd)............................ .10 1.00
> A beautiful ruffled white, with violet purple penciling on lower petals. A fine ruffled variety.

IMMENSITY .... .25 2.50
> Tall, strong plant. Bright salmon color. Very large flowers and many open at a time. Very choice. One of Kunderd's prize winers.

INDIAN SUMMER (Kunderd)............................ .50 5.00
> A very massive ruffled variety of light lavender rose-pink on white ground. A beautiful flower. Late bloomer.

INDIAN MAID (Kunderd).................................. .10 1.00
> A fine peach blossom pink, with beautiful darker throat. Very choice and distinct.

JEWELL (Zee) .... .15 1.50
> A beautiful salmon pink with a clear golden yellow throat. A good sized flower which does not show any signs of the primulinis type.

EUGENE LEFEBRE

DESCRIPTION ON PAGE SEVEN

	EACH	DOZEN
JENNY LIND (Decorah Glad Gardens)	$ .25	$2.50

The blossoms are the purest, softest shrimp pink, deepening to geranium pink at tips of petals. Throat beautiful, creamy yellow, with blotch of light yellow on reverse side of lower petals. As one lady exclaimed, this is a darling and should be in every collection.

	EACH	DOZEN
JEAN DeTAILLES (Lemoine)	.20	2.00

A French introduction. Deep salmon flaked deeper, and with maroon throat. No mistake was ever made in growing this flower. Enormous flowers on tall spike. A georgeous variety

	EACH	DOZEN
J. T. PIRIE (Kunderd)	.25	2.50

A sort of mahogany brown with remarkable yellow bordered dark mahogany-brown throat. In a class by itself and should be in every collection.

	EACH	DOZEN
JOY	.15	1.50

	EACH	DOZEN
LE MARECHAL FOCH (VanDeursen)	.07	.75

One of the largest of the light pinks, and one of the best of the Holland introductions. Early.

	EACH	DOZEN
LOVELINESS	.10	1.00

All that its name implies. A light creamy yellow, with a tinge of apricot. Flowers large, and a general favorite.

	EACH	DOZEN
LOUISE (Wright)	.15	1.50

A most beautiful lavender. Large flower, four and five inches across. Bright lavender, lighter toward center, blotch of velvety maroon down center. A prize winner.

	EACH	DOZEN
LILLIAN WEBB (Diener)	.15	1.50

Strawberry pink with carmine velvety center, overlaid with maroon and brownish stripes. The stems are slender and give the appearance of a lily.

	EACH	DOZEN
LONGFELLOW (Decorah Glad Gardens)	.50	5.00

LaFrance pink. A wonderfully pleasing color. Many large, wide open flowers. Tall, slender, wiry stem. Excellent for cutting. Has made a great hit the last two seasons.

	EACH	DOZEN
LUCETTE (Bill's)	.10	1.00

Pure white except back of petals carry a trace of phlox pink, which imparts an alluring orchid sheen to the flowers. Lower petals also have a dainty subdued feather of soft phlox pink.

GOLD

DESCRIPTION ON PAGE EIGHT

EACH   DOZEN

LOS ANGELES (Houdyshel)..............................$ .35 $3.50
A charming variety. Shrimp-pink, tinted orange, with an orange tinted stripe in throat. A cut-and-come-again variety. Something unusual, and a wonderful cut flower.

MARIETTA (Metzner) .... .35   3.50
A winner among the salmon colored varieties. Large, soft salmon pink, with a pleasing blotch of darker shade in throat.

MARIE KUNDERD (Kunderd)....................... .20   2.00
Conceded to be the best pure white ruffled cariety. Early.

MASTERPIECE (Kunderd) .... .25   2.50
A large size bloom of American beauty rose color. Beautifully ruffled. Exquisite and Mrs. Arthur are better, and same color.

MARY FENNELL (Kunderd)....................... .10   1.00
A beautiful light lavender tinged with soft pink. Has soft primrose yellow throat. Flowers large and wide open. A most delicately colored flower.

MARSHAL FOCH (Kunderd)....................... .15   1.50
The king of the pinks. Ruffled flowers of large size. A beautiful salmon pink, striped with a deeper salmon toward edge of petals. Don't fail to grow this variety.

MRS. DR. NORTON (Kunderd)....................... .10   1.00
This variety heads the list in the light pink class. Light pink in color, shading to a yellow center. An exquisite combination in colors.

MRS. FRANK PENDLETON (Kunderd)............... .07   .75
Large flowers of delicate pink with large blotch of deep red in throat. An old variety, but hard to beat.

MRS. FRANCIS KING (Coblentz)....................... .05   .50
One of the old standbys. Orange scarlet blend. Very large flowers nicely placed on tall, stately spikes. Fine decorative variety.

MRS. H. E. BOTHIN (Diener)....................... .15   1.50
Light geranium pink, heavily ruffled. Tall, straight spikes. A lovely combination, and do not fail to include this in your collection.

	EACH	DOZEN

MRS. LEON DOUGLAS (Diener) ....$ .50 $5.00
 Winner of many prizes for the largest bloom in exist-
 ance. Ground color begonia rose, striped with flame
 and scarlet. Lip pale lemon. This without exception
 is one of Diener's best productions.

MURIEL (Pfitzer) .... .15 1.50
 From a few feet distance it would be difficult to dis-
 tinguish any difference between this variety and Ger-
 aldine Farrar. A true lilac blue, slightly darker at tips
 of petals.

MING TOY (Kunderd) .... .15 1.50
 One of the worth-while primulinus varieties. Very
 large flower with deep buff-yellow throat. Buff in
 color, and very odd and unique. Fine.

MISS MAUD FAY (Diener) .... .25 2.50
 Pale Amaranth pink with a light stripe running thru
 the center of each petal. The edges of the petals shade
 into Tyrian pink. Flowers are very open and large.

MARY PICKFORD (Kunderd) .... .15 1.50
 Flower and spike of most delicate creamy white.
 Throat finest, soft sulphur yellow. Stem and calix
 also white.

MRS. ARTHUR MEEKER (Kunderd) .... .25 2.50
 Exceptionally fine, rich deep American beauty color.
 A very beautiful and unusual variety.

MRS. WATT (Crawford) .... .10 1.00
 Beautiful clear wine red. Fine flower, and strong,
 vigorous grower.

MRS. JOHN R. WALSH (Diener) .... .25 2.50
 Heavily ruffled flesh pink. Three lower petals of
 flame scarlet, shading into dark ruby in the throat.
 Flowers very large.

MRS. F. C. PETERS (Fischer) .... .25 2.50
 Fine rosy lilac blossoms with softest crimson blotch,
 and many open at one time. Resembles an orchid in
 color. A choice variety which everyone admires.

NANCY HANKS (Salbach) .... .50 5.00
 Very rich peach red to orange pink with prominent
 grenadine tongue. Wide open flowers much on the
 order of Alice Tiplady, but larger and of taller
 growth. Also slightly lighter in color.

	EACH	DOZEN
ORANGE GLORY (Kunderd) $	.15	$1.50

Beautiful, intensely ruffled orange colored blossoms with lighter throat. A very rich and striking color. Wonderful variety.

POLLYANNA (Decorah Glad Gardens) .25   2.50

A clear yellow and nicely ruffled. A beauty.

PRINCE OF WALES (Holland) .07   .75

Softest salmon with an apricot undertone. Still leads as one of the best salmon color varieties.

PERSIA (National Bulb Farms) .25   2.50

A rich, deep, mahogany black-red, buds almost black. Its unusual color immediately attracts attention, and it is the most popular variety we are growing.

PINK CLOUD (Kunderd) .75   7.50

A large, distinct and showy ruffled variety. Usually from five to seven soft rose-pink blooms open at one time. A very beautiful deep rose throat.

PELLA (Kunderd) .15   1.50

Very beautiful early rose-pink. Very good.

PINK WONDER (Coleman) .10   1.00

An exceptionally large light pink. You will like this one.

PRIDE OF HILLEGOM (Holland) .10   1.00

Very beautiful scarlet. Large flowers well placed on spike.

PRIDE OF LANCASTER (Kunderd) .15   1.50

Beautiful brilliant orange-salmon, with a deeper orange throat. Very nicely ruffled.

PURPLE GLORY (Kunderd) .25   2.50

A beautiful ruffled variety. Deepest velvety maroon red, with blotches almost black. Gorgeous, and a variety you will be proud to display.

PYTHIA .15   1.50

A very large, bright red, and one of the finest of its color.

PEARL OF CALIFORNIA (Kingsley) 10.00

Soft LaFrance pink, blending to a rosy white throat. Each spike contains from 25 to 32 buds. Flowers five inches in diameter.

PINK PERFECTION (Hopman) .15   1.50

A very bright pink, self color. Flowers perfectly placed on a long wiry stem, but has a fault of many spikes coming crooked.

JEAN DeTALLIES

DESCRIPTION ON PAGE ELEVEN

	EACH	DOZEN

RICHARD DIENER (Diener) ....$ .35 $3.50
A pure geranium pink with a sprinkling of light ruby
in the creamy yellow center. Large flowers and many
open at a time. Large, graceful spike and a sensation
in the pink class.

ROMANCE (Kunderd) .... .25   2.50
Large orange, salmon-rose, red and yellow throat.
Wine blue bordered petals. An unusual and odd col-
ored beauty.

ROSE ASH (Diener) .... .15   1.50
Extra strong, large plant. Corinthian red shading
into ashes of roses on the outer edges. Lower petals
light yellow speckled with ruby. Flowers large, and
a variety that is sure to please you.

1910 ROSE (Kunderd) .... .10   1.00
Deep rose-pink shading to rose-red. Lower petals
slightly mottled at times. White center line. First
to bloom and a very popular florist variety.

SANFORD, or Queen of the Night (Metzner) .... .75   7.50
Deep maroon, almost black. Very large flower.

SALMON BEAUTY (Kunderd) .... .10   1.00
One of the few primulinus varieties we consider worth
growing. Deep salmon with salmon yellow throat.
Nice size flowers on a tall, straight spike.

SCARLANO (Kunderd) .... .15   1.50
Light, bright orange-red. Finely ruffled. A large
number of these in bloom looks like a bon-fire.

SCARLET PINCEPS (Kunderd) .... .15   1.50
Large scarlet, self color. Beautiful, and a variety
you should grow.

SCARLET WONDER (Groff) .... .25   2.50
Mammoth, pure deep scarlet flowers on tall, straight
spike. This variety is conceded to be the largest scarlet to date.

SWEET LAVENDER (Coleman) .... .20   2.00
An exceptionally fine early variety. Light lavender,
deeper in throat, with purple blotch. A beauty.

SUNSET (Diener) .... .10   1.00
A very early coral pink, and a very lovely variety.
Large flowers.

SYDONIA (Holland) .... .10   1.00
A most unique and distinctive flower. Violet, slightly
lighter in throat.

SWEET LAVENDER

DESCRIPTION ON PAGE SEVENTEEN

	EACH	DOZEN

SANS PARIEL (Vilmorin) .... $ .75 $7.50
Apricot pink with white throat. Large flower and perfectly gorgeous.

SULPHUR GLOW (Kunderd) .... .10   1.00
A beautiful shade of yellow. Many well expanded, intensely ruffled flowers open at one time.

SIR ROGER CASEMENT (Diener) .... .15   1.50

TYRIAN BEAUTY (Kunderd) .... .25   2.50
Magnificent spike of large flowers of pure Tyrian rose, near American beauty rose. Upper petals slightly lighter. Tall, strong grower, and it has no competition in this color.

TYCO ZANG (Austin) 1-inch bulbs 1.50   15.00
Blooms are of a beautiful salmon pink, with a brilliance unsurpassed and possibly unequaled under electric lights. Flower usually measures 5 inches in diameter and has several blooms open at one time. Grand new variety you ought to have.

VEILED BRILLIANCE (Austin) 7.50
Brilliant blooms of salmon-pink with creamy throat, tinted grayish blue, having the appearance of being thinly veiled. Wonderful effect, new and different. Flowers 5 to 6 inches in diameter and ten open at a time. Increases well.

WILBRINK (Holland) .... .10   1.00
This is a sport of Halley and as early as Halley. It is a creamy pink with soft yellow blotch on lower petals. A distinctive flower.

WHITE GIANT (VanMeerbeek) .... .15   1.50
Very large flowers of pure white. Resembles an Easter lily. Very good.

WHITE GLORY (Kunderd) .... .15   1.50
Lovers of the ruffled type of blooms will fall in love with this one. Georgeous ivory white with a touch of iris-blue in throat. Fine as a delicate iris.

W. H. PHIPPS (Diener) 1.00   10.00
One of the most beautiful flowers ever produced by Diener. LaFrance pink overlaid with light rose-salmon. Lower petals delicately striped with ruby. Enormous flowers, tall spikes, and as many as 16 to 20 blooms open at once.

KINDLY NOTE

O N account of receiving numerous inquiries from many of our friends, as to whether we could supply them with tulip, hyacinth or hardy lily bulbs, we have finally made arrangements with a large wholesale bulb company to enable us to furnish you tulips of the standard varieties in quantities of 25 or more, hyacinths, 12 or more and hardy lilies six or more. These quantities must be of one variety, however.

We do not issue a list of varieties of the bulbs mentioned above, or make prices, but you may make your selection from any flower catalog, write us the quantity you wish, and we will quote you the wholesale prices delivered.

Orders should be received not later than October 10th, as these bulbs should be planted not later than November 1st, and can be planted as early as September 20th.

DELPHINIUM

We expect to plant several thousand of the famous Wrexham and Hollyhock strains of Delphinium, the finest strains ever produced. The original stock was imported from England, and is considered the best in the world. This is a hardy perennial and one of the most popular of the hardy flowers.

Woodlawn Gardens

E. C. SWARTLEY, Proprietor

STERLING, ILLINOIS

GROWERS OF NEW AND STANDARD

GLADIOLI

WHOLESALE PRICE LIST

Price per 1000 unless otherwise noted.   250 at 1000 rate.   Write for price on Bulblets.

	No. 1	No. 2	No. 3	No. 4	No. 5
Annie Eberius	$25.00	$20.00	$16.00	$12.00	$9.00
B. Smith	35.00	30.00	....	....	....
Carmen Sylvia	30.00	25.00	20.00	15.00	10.00
Crimson Glow	25.00	20.00	16.00	....	....
E. Faber (per 100)	8.00	6.50	5.00	4.00	3.00
Eugene Lefebre (per 100)	8.00	6.50	5.00	4.00	....
Glendale (per 100)	4.00	3.00	2.50	2.00	....
Gold (per 100)	5.00	4.00	3.25	....	....
Marshall Foch (per 100)	5.00	4.00	....	....	....
Mrs. Dr. Norton	25.00	20.00	....	....	....
Mrs. H. E. Bothin	30.00	25.00	20.00	15.00	10.00
Pink Wonder	30.00	25.00	20.00	15.00	10.00
Rose Ash	30.00	25.00	20.00	15.00	10.00
Sweet Lavender (per 100)	4.00	3.25	....	....	....
Scarlet Wonder (per 100)	....	....	5.00	4.00	3.20

Please send pricelist

SPECIAL COLLECTIONS

COLLECTION No. 1—$1.00

2	Evelyn Kirtland	$ .20
2	Carmen Sylvia	.30
2	Byron Smith	.24
2	Flora	.20
1	Rose Ash	.15
2	Pink Wonder	.20

$1.29

COLLECTION No. 2—$1.00

2	Sweet Lavender	$ .30
2	Gold	.40
2	Mrs. Dr. Norton	.20
2	Pink Wonder	.20
1	Hoosier	.20

$1.30

COLLECTION No. 3—$2.00

2	Hoosier	$ .40
3	White Giant	.45
2	Romance	.50
2	Persia	.50
2	Alice Tiplady	.20
2	Glendale	.30

$2.35

COLLECTION No. 4—$2.00

2	Tyrian Beauty	$ .40
2	Marshal Foch	.30
2	Marie Kunderd	.30
2	Glendale	.30
1	Mrs. Leon Douglas	.50
3	Gold	.60

$2.40

COLLECTION No. 5—$3.00

3	Eugene LeFebre	$ .75
2	Jean DuTailles	.60
3	Tyrian Beauty	.60
2	Purple Glory	.50
2	Persia	.50
2	Romance	.50

$3.45

COLLECTION No. 6—$5.00

1	Tyco Zang	$1.50
1	Break O'Day	2.00
1	Stanford	.75
1	Sans Pariel	.75
2	Los Angeles	.70

$5.70

Fine varieties of mixed bulbs, per 100 .... $3.00

THE GIFT BOX

SPECIAL PRICE OF $1.00

We are making up a special gift box which contains the greatest value we have ever offered in a collection of "glad" varieties. This box contains 15 distinct varieties of our most popular blooms (not named), and to the novice in growing gladiolus this collection will be a revelation.

As an Easter remembrance, or as a gift to mother on Mother's Day, there is no other gift which could possibly give greater pleasure, and would also be a kind reminder of the donor when the "glads" are in bloom.

This collection will be packed in a very attractive box, and the wrapper will display the blooms in colors identical with the colors on our catalog.

A number of church societies and woman's clubs have taken advantage of our offer to dispose of gladiolus, and have realized some very nice profits from the sale of our bulbs. If you will write us for particulars, we will be very glad to give you full details.